*Harbor House Ministries, Inc., is a multiethnic, interdenominational, Christian outreach that provides spiritual, economic, and educational development opportunities to children, youth, and families so that together we can become all that God intends us to be. Harbor House is supported by donors and volunteers from many sectors of the community and welcomes people of all ethnic and religious backgrounds. We do not require a faith commitment in exchange for any of our services. Staff, volunteers, and participants represent all the major racial and ethnic populations of our surrounding community. People of all ages and backgrounds contribute to Harbor House, giving of their time, talent, and resources. One older Mien woman shares her fresh garden greens with Harbor House and contributes cash each month toward the water bill for her part in our community garden. Support from foundations and donations of time by volunteer professionals make it possible for Harbor House to spend resources directly on program participants. We welcome you to join this very large family. We'll help you to think of a unique way to contribute. For further information about Harbor House or InnerCity Expressions, please contact Harbor House Ministries, Inc., at 510-534-0165. You are welcome to visit or write to us at 1811 Eleventh Ave., Oakland, CA 94606 and to visit our web site at www.hhministries.org.*

# ABOUT THE PHOTOGRAPHER

Marianne Thomas is a photo editor at the *San Francisco Chronicle,* as well as an instructor at the Academy of Art College in San Francisco. She has shown her photographs in numerous art exhibitions. Marianne was a general winner in the 2000 M.I.L.K. International Photographic Competition judged by Elliott Erwitt and received an Award of Excellence in the 1998 Pictures of the Year newspaper Picture-Editing Portfolio. One of her photographs is in the School of Communications collection at the University of Miami. She received a B.S. in journalism with a minor in Latin American studies from Syracuse University in New York and has traveled widely throughout the world.

# CONTENTS

# FOREWORD

The children in this book personify the beauty and power of racial and ethnic diversity. In stunning photographs by Marianne Thomas, they express themselves openly and unselfconsciously, the way only children can. Their faces come in all colors and shades, representing 38 nationalities. While Oakland has a reputation for diversity, these pictures show a medley of cultures that is breathtaking. In several cases, the medley is within one family: Native American, Filipino, and Hawaiian, for example, in one beautiful mixture.

In their own words, the children share their love of homeland traditions along with more newly acquired tastes of their adopted country—in one case, traditional Greek dance and basketball. They see their heritage as something that makes them unique, as well as something to share with their friends. Several children said they are learning the languages of their friends. A Laotian girl is learning to speak Spanish and Thai.

Through these children, we see differences between people and cultures and don't have to be afraid of them or pretend they don't exist. They do, and they're gorgeous and exhilarating. We are free to appreciate and celebrate our differences, as well as the emotions or experiences we have in common. We see the unadulterated joy of two friends laughing as they swing, the seriousness of a 5-year-old having his tie straightened before a Cinco de Mayo celebration, the excitement—mixed with a touch of apprehension—of a girl going to her First Holy Communion in the fancy white dress her mother made her.

This book also includes a fascinating list of cultural traditions from the ethnicities and countries represented. We learn that in Colombia during Desfile de los Silleteros ("The Carriers' Parade"), artisans weave flowers into tapestries that tell stories. And that during India's Festival of Lights, Diwali, families light candles and oil lamps, exchange gifts, go to the temple, and set off fireworks to celebrate the return of the Hindu deity Lord Rama after 14 years of exile.

With this publication, Harbor House holds up a mirror to Oakland's remarkable multicultural face so we can see it for what it is. Oaklanders are so accustomed to our racial diversity and harmony we often take it for granted, but many of us have long believed the city can serve as a model for the rest of the nation still trying to figure out how to live together. This book is a perfect promotion of what Oakland can share with the country and the world.

I fell in love with the book, its subjects, and its creators. I'm sure you will, too. It is a treasure that shows off the unique and most appealing characteristic of our city—our diversity—with the irresistible faces of children of the world, right here in our world, Oakland.

Brenda Payton
Columnist, *Oakland Tribune*

# PREFACE

Some years ago I purchased a small, black-and-white photographic book of children from around the world. The book actually portrayed children from very few countries, fewer even than the number of countries represented in the Lower San Antonio neighborhood of Oakland surrounding Harbor House, the Christian outreach where I work. The 1990 census reported more than 66 different ethnic groups living in Oakland, making it one of the most diverse communities in the United States. Comparing that slim book of photographs with Harbor House newsletter images of our neighborhood children in all their glorious differences, I dreamed of someday producing a photographic coffee-table book that would show off the beauty and diversity of Oakland through its youngest inhabitants.

Creating InnerCity Expressions, a youth graphic arts business, in 1995 was the first step I took toward realizing my dream. This business, run by Harbor House with help from volunteer professionals, trains teens in skills such as computer graphics, marketing, accounting, printing, photography, interviewing, and writing. The teens produce flyers, newsletters, business cards, and other graphic arts services for Harbor House and outside agencies.

InnerCity Expressions incorporated my goal for this book in a seminal project called Children of Oakland that has provided multiple opportunities for the teens to learn professional skills. The teens who worked on the project—Takena Feazell, Mercedes Gibson, Katie Khanthavong, Arnell Pleasants, and Lai Saelee—helped set up photo shoots, interviewed virtually all the child subjects for the book, transcribed the interviews, and helped with planning and marketing. They even won a grant to purchase a computer for creating graphic art. This type of work experience stands in stark contrast to the general lack of career-enhancing jobs available for our urban youth. Such opportunities have a lifetime benefit. I believe that when teens are exposed to experiences that allow them to discover their innate, God-given gifts, they will be motivated to pursue their education and seek further opportunities toward a meaningful career.

I deeply appreciate the cooperation of the children and families who gave life to this book, and I am ever grateful to our photographer, Marianne Thomas, who worked tirelessly with InnerCity Expressions to c[illegible] children in all their individuality. Marianne has produced a stunn[illegible] of art that is not only a celebration of differences, but also of what [illegible] have in common. "As the project progressed," Marianne told me, "I n[illegible]ced that no matter what the background of the children, they had such joyous spirits. I tried to cover the spectrum of the childhood experience as it unfolded for me so that, together, the photos made a statement about being a child."

I am also grateful to the many other professionals and businesspeople who helped me refine the project and supported my desire to make it the best quality: Keith Criss, of Keith Criss Illustrations, who made himself available from the beginning of the project as an adviser and who designed the *Children of Oakland 2000* calendar and brochure; Denise Goldman, of Ten Celsius Communication Design, who created the graceful, poetic design for the book; and Julie Harris, for her hours upon hours of editing. Finally, I am grateful to the staff and board of Harbor House for their supportive work and for allowing me the freedom to form InnerCity Expressions and Children of Oakland.

Harbor House would like to express special thanks to the financial supporters of InnerCity Expressions when it was in its formative stages and contributors to the Children of Oakland project, especially Business Design Associates, Global Ministries of First Presbyterian Church of Berkeley, the McCray Family Foundation, Moraga Valley Presbyterian Church, the Wayne & Gladys Valley Foundation, the Y&H Soda Foundation, and individual supporters of Harbor House. All proceeds from the sale of the book will support InnerCity Expressions and Harbor House programs.

It has been a privilege and an honor to meet and learn from each of the different people involved in this project. All the beauty, diversity, and talent of the people you see and read about in these pages has been created by God the Almighty. May He be glorified through this work.

Mary M. Biasotti
Director of Economic Development, Harbor House Ministries, Inc.

*The Children of Oakland*

# *samoan*

## DANIKKO TAYLOR, AGE 6

*Danniko honors his Samoan heritage by participating in a family dance group.*
*He comes from a line of high chiefs,*
*and his name means "brave man" in the Samoan language.*

*"Samoa is like here," Danikko says, "but in Samoa you don't have to pay bills*
*or anything. You have to find your own food.*
*We had a lot of chickens, pigs, bats, and cows, and we made our houses out of sticks."*

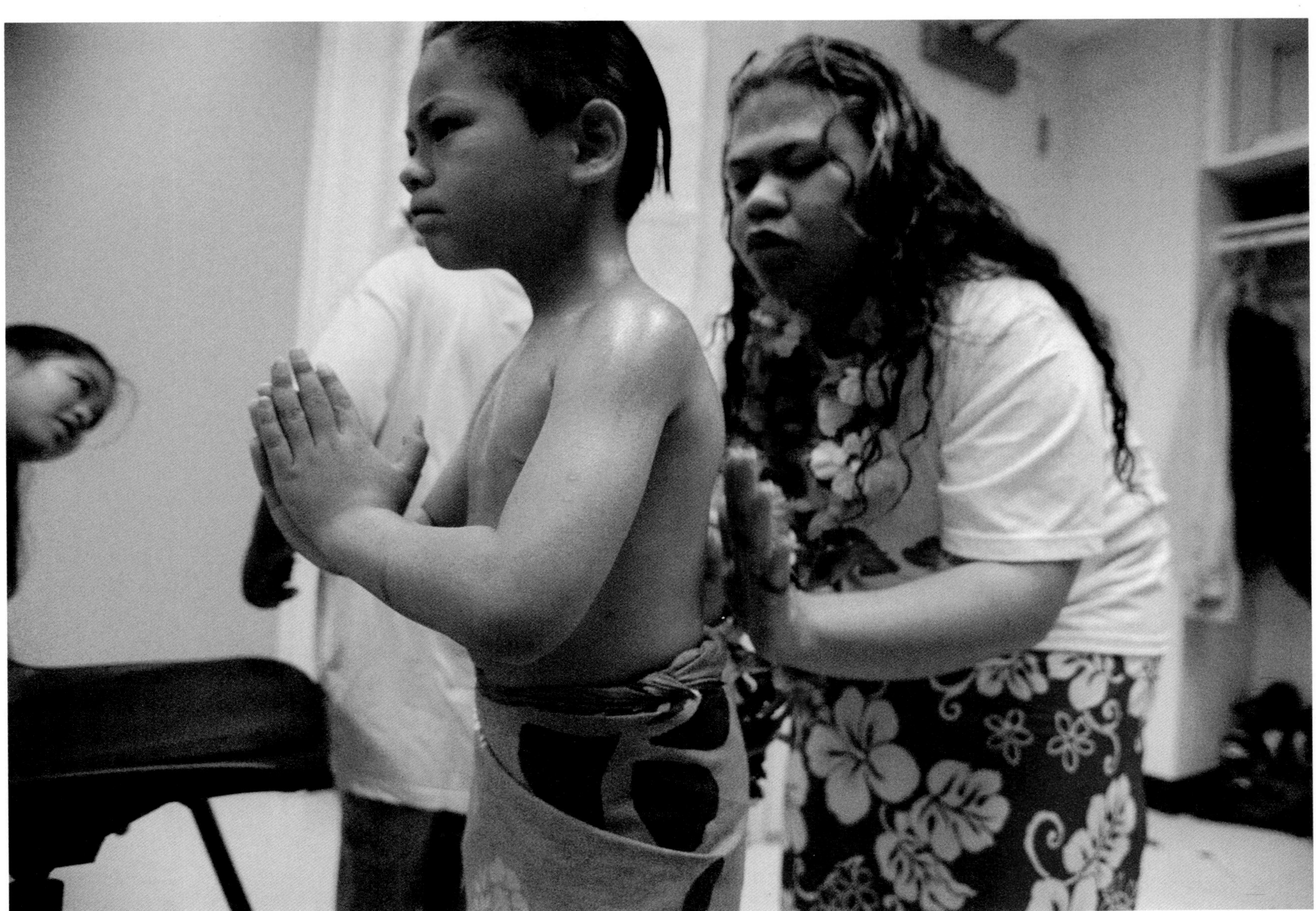

# *trinidadian*

MERISSA LYONS, AGE 9

*Merissa (far left) appreciates the natural aspects of both Oakland and Trinidad. "Oakland has a lot of pretty places, like parks with flowers, and big waterfalls. In Trinidad, it's way too hot, but the water is warm when it rains, and there are a lot of beaches." Merissa also enjoys the food of her native country and leading dances in Carnival. But if she could live anywhere, she says, "I'd live in a dessert factory."*

# *german*

Finn T. Liss, age 8

*Finn says he likes Oakland better than Germany "because the sun shines most of the time here." However, he misses Germany's winter snow and tobogganing.*

*His favorite food, Maultaschen ("mouth pockets"), a regional specialty of Stuttgart, is somewhat like ravioli served in soup.*
*Finn also likes to play drums with a friend and practice piano. His friends are Chinese, African, Japanese, and Turkish.*

*During Cinco de Mayo,*
*Miguel participates*
*in school performances*
*and helps his mom make tamales.*
*His favorite*
*aspect of the celebration*
*is the food.*

*"When I grow up,*
*I want to be a police officer,"*
*Miguel says.*
*Officers at Miguel's school*
*who stop traffic*
*to let children safely cross the street*
*are his inspiration.*
*"I want to take care of kids*
*so they don't get hit by cars."*

# mexican

MIGUEL NUÑO, AGE 6

*Not everyone at school*
*can do a tootsie roll on the*
*monkey bars,*
*but she can, says Annie*
*(at far left and*
*at right on facing page).*

*"School is also fun*
*because we get to do math*
*every day, and math*
*is my favorite subject.*
*One of my friends, Maddie,*
*is from Brazil just like me.*
*She has short, little curly hair*
*and darker skin."*

## *brazilian*

ANNIE STOREY, AGE 6

SCHOOL'S
ANNUAL
USA

MOO SOOLSA

# *korean*

## April Kim, age 10, and Sean Kim, age 12

*Whether she's practicing*
*the Korean martial art tae kwon do*
*or choosing a favorite food,*
*April has her own way*
*of expressing herself, and*
*she appreciates*
*unique qualities in others as well.*
*"No one else is exactly like me,"*
*she says. "Everyone is different."*

*Her older brother, Sean,*
*is proud that his Korean heritage*
*is part of what defines him:*
*"I like how rich the Korean culture is.*
*I like the language.*
*There are so many different kinds*
*of clothing and food."*
*Sean also practices tae kwon do*
*and likes to play a traditional Korean*
*game called Yoot noli.*

# *filipino*

Jeffrey Andrade, age 8

*"After school I like to stay and read books,*
*like history books and a book about virtues," says Jeffrey.*
*"At home I don't read too much*
*because I get busy with chores and all.*

*"If I could change one thing about my neighborhood,*
*I would clean it up, especially the leaves and the cans.*
*For the world,*
*what I hope for is a lot of peace, so everything could change."*

# bosnian

### Sanda Isakovic, age 6

*Sanda (far left, at her sixth birthday party)*
*has fond memories of Bosnia from before the war.*
*"In Bosnia, it felt good, it was nice,*
*the houses were nice. I felt sad leaving."*
*But she likes living in Oakland now.*
*She's particularly happy walking to school*
*with her 8-year-old sister, Selma (far right),*
*and their Spanish-speaking, Cambodian, and Bosnian friends.*

# *nigerian*

## Edosa Enagbare-Ona, age 5

*"I like to study math,*
*draw, and paint,*
*and I like playing soccer*
*so that I can*
*get the trophy,"*
*says Edosa (at far left,*
*with his brothers,*
*and on facing page).*

*"When I grow up*
*I want to be a school teacher*
*so I can be a good person."*

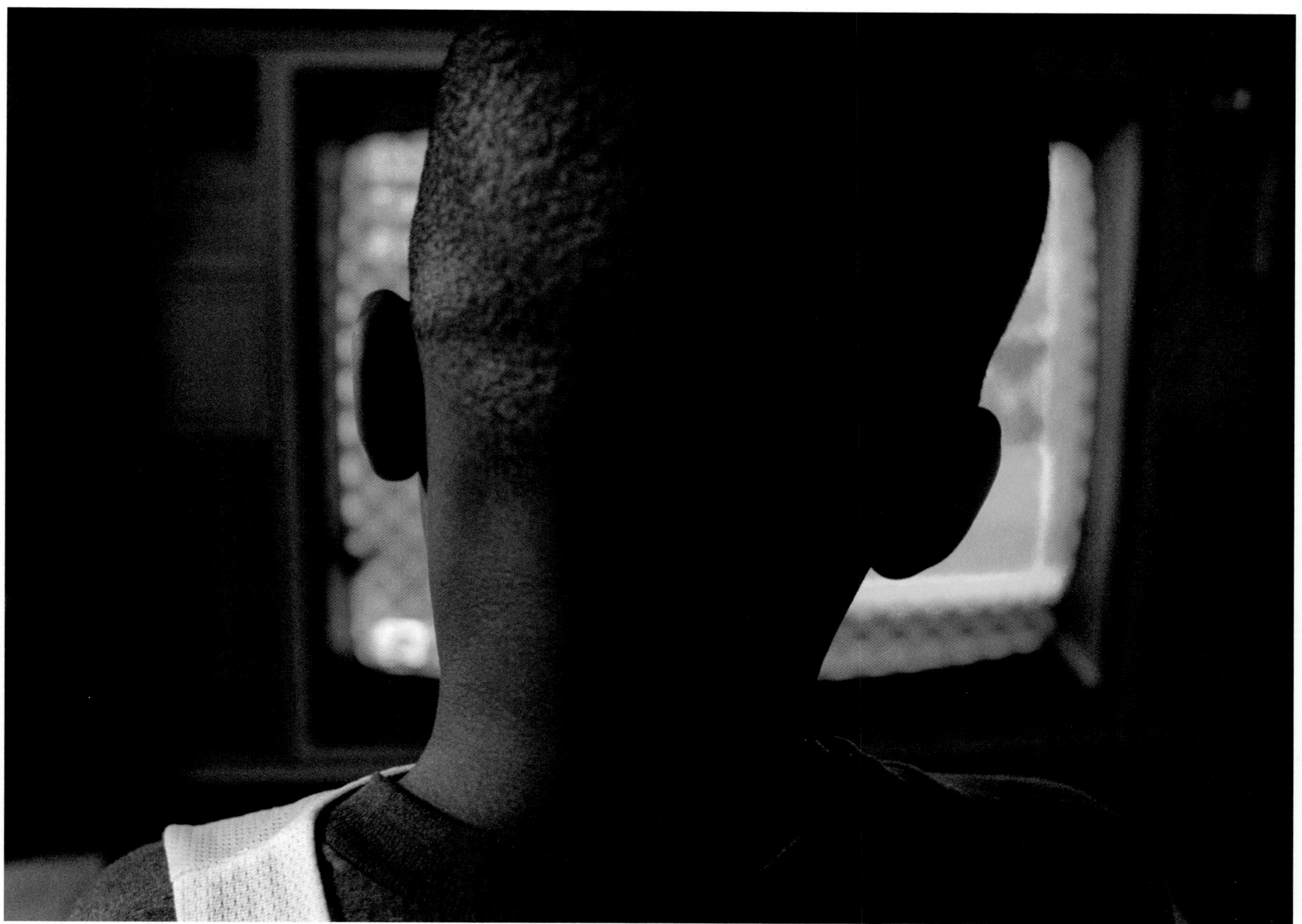

ATH
FIELD
HELLO
ST. JARLAT
TRACK &

# *belizean*

## Jennifer Hyde, age 6

*Jennifer (far left)*
*has two favorite activities*
*at her school,*
*St. Jarlath's:*
*reading time,*
*especially when the book is*
The Good Bad Cat;
*and math.*
*She also likes homework*
*("because you get stars").*
*When she's not at school,*
*Jennifer likes to play*
*the card game Go Fish.*
*"It's a lot of fun*
*and only a little hard."*

*If she could change*
*anything in the world,*
*Jennifer says,*
*"I would want every town*
*to be a happy town,*
*so people wouldn't fight*
*with each other."*

# *gambian*

BAKARY MILON, AGE 5

*Bakary speaks four languages*
*—Jola, Mandinka, and Wolof, as well as English—*
*and enjoys playing the* djimbe *(drum).*

*When he grows up,*
*he wants to be "like a man who delivers mattresses*
*so people can have beds and stuff when night comes around."*

Where Do Monsters Live?
Five Little Monsters
Whose
Forest
Underground

# *guatemalan, colombian*

## Tony Young, age 8, and Marcela Young, age 11

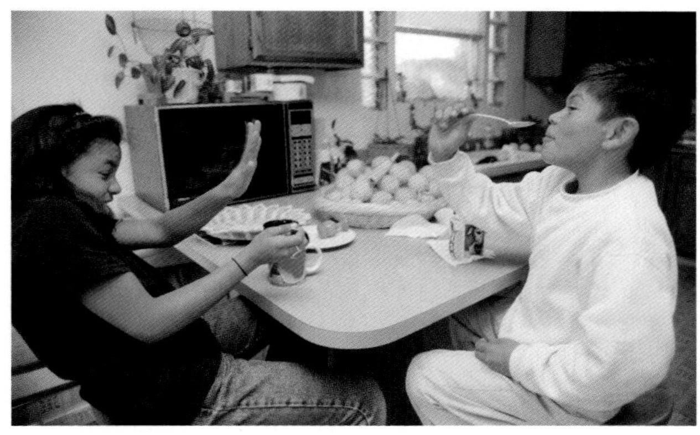

*Tony, from Guatemala,*
*and his sister, Marcela, from Colombia,*
*both want to work*
*in public service when they grow up.*

*"It makes me feel bad*
*that some people care only for themselves," says Marcela.*
*"I want to be a police officer.*
*I've seen a lot of shows where they're helping people out."*

*"What do I want to be when I grow up?*
*Oh, that's easy," says Tony.*
*"A fireman, because I want to help people*
*when their houses burn down."*

# *salvadoran*

WILMER ANTONIO CALLEJAS, AGE 10

*"In El Salvador, everyone speaks only Spanish," says Wilmer.*
*"Here, everyone is from different countries*
*and we need to learn English. It's hard to learn English."*

*Despite the challenges*
*of adjusting to life in Oakland, Wilmer says he likes the hills here,*
*cars, playing soccer, and playing Nintendo.*

# *mien*

## Nai Saechao, age 9

*"My favorite day*
*is Friday,"*
*says Nai (middle),*
*"because*
*there's no school*
*the next day."*
*Still, she is*
*looking forward*
*to getting*
*a good education*
*because*
*"I want to go to college*
*so I can*
*make money."*
*Math is her*
*favorite subject.*

# *eastern european jewish*

## Ilana Hannah Wexler, age 8

*Ilana enjoys both the "fun noise" of her Oakland neighborhood and the quiet of the Jewish Shabbat, or Sabbath, which she says "is like peace to me."*

*If she could be granted any wish, it would be to live forever —"and to be a grown-up, because grown-ups get to do anything."*

# *cambodian*

Ryan Kong, age 8

*"Oakland is cool," says Ryan (far left).*
*"I like all the Oakland teams—the Raiders, the A's, the Warriors—*
*because Oakland is my hometown.*
*When they win, I get excited. When they lose, I'm sad.*

*"In Oakland, I can make friends easily.*
*I learn different languages, like Chinese and Spanish.*
*In Oakland, we need to add more houses,*
*though, so that the homeless can live in them."*

# *indian*

RAHUL SINGH RAO, AGE 8

*Rahul (shown here at his father's restaurant) has exhibited an adventurous spirit from the age of 2, when he walked by himself to a park three blocks away.*

*Now that he's older, his love of adventure often expresses itself through his choice of books and games.*

*"My favorite reading subject is Harry Potter," he says,*

*"and I like chess because it's like fighting, but with wood or plastic."*

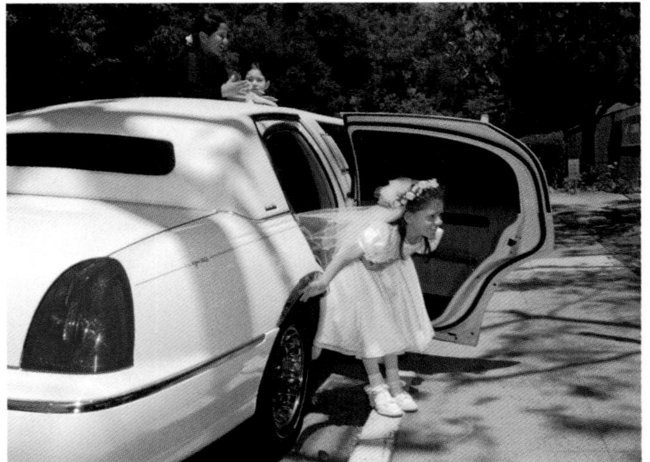

# *nicaraguan*

NIQUIRANA HICKS RODRIGUEZ, AGE 9

*"Taking my very first host*
*[communion bread representing the body of Jesus]*
*in my hand,*
*I felt excitement, joyful, happy*
*because I was waiting for years*
*to have my First Holy Communion,"*
*says Niki.*
*"I liked my dress*
*because my mom made it.*
*I felt fancy."*

*Niki appreciates that Nicaraguans are*
*just one of many different kinds of people in Oakland.*
*"I feel kind of excited knowing other people,*
*knowing what's special about them," she says.*
*"I can learn*
*different stuff and different cultures."*

# *thai*

ABBY BOUAPHAVONG, AGE 10

*"Oakland is not ghetto,"*
*says Abby.*
*"It's okay. It's cool to hang out.*
*You can meet a lot of people.*
*I have Black,*
*White, Asian, and Native American friends*
*who are like*
*brothers and sisters.*
*They are always there for me."*

# *liberian*

TERISHA CHARLENE HARRIS, AGE 11

*Terisha (at left on facing page and below)*
*shows joyful confidence in herself and her unique qualities.*
*What makes her different from anyone else,*
*she says, is that she's "beautiful and real affectionate."*

*An experience she will remember forever was when she saved her sister's life.*
*"A lady at church was backing out*
*of the parking lot, and I grabbed my sister out of the way."*

*Talia (left)*
*is the consummate creator.*
*"If I paint something*
*and I mess up,*
*then I make something else out of it,"*
*she says.*
*"In science, I'm learning to make stuff,*
*to make things work.*
*Once I made a basketball and*
*basketball hoop."*

*She also loves animals.*
*"I want to be a veterinarian*
*when I grow up*
*because I want to take care of pets*
*and make them feel better."*

# *paraguayan*

TALIA CHESS, AGE 6

# *eritrean*

ROABEL MEDHANIE, AGE 7

*"If I could change anything,*
*it would be the war in Eritrea,"*
*says Roabel.*
*"It's bad.*
*When I think about it...*
*guns and stuff...*
*I don't want*
*to be near them.*
*It's just about land*
*—they're bigger;*
*they're being selfish.*

*"When I grow up*
*I want to be a basketball player*
*or a lawyer.*
*Or maybe a judge.*
*I like to talk,*
*and it looks fun*
*—one judge on TV*
*acts really funny.*
*My biggest wish is to be rich*
*and have lots of friends.*
*It's no fun*
*if you have no friends."*

# *chinese-japanese-vietnamese*

## Derrick Tsuyuki Cooc, age 8, and Hope Setsuko Cooc, age 7

*The Coocs identify with three cultures, and the children participate in games and customs that honor them all.*

*Derrick (above, second from left) enjoys speaking the different languages. "I get to speak Vietnamese, Chinese, and Japanese with my mom sometimes, my dad sometimes, and my sister, too."*

*Hope (above, third from left, and on facing page) says, "I like Chinese lion dancing and playing Chinese jump rope. On Japanese New Year, I like to dress up in a Japanese kimono, wear slippers, and put my hair up."*

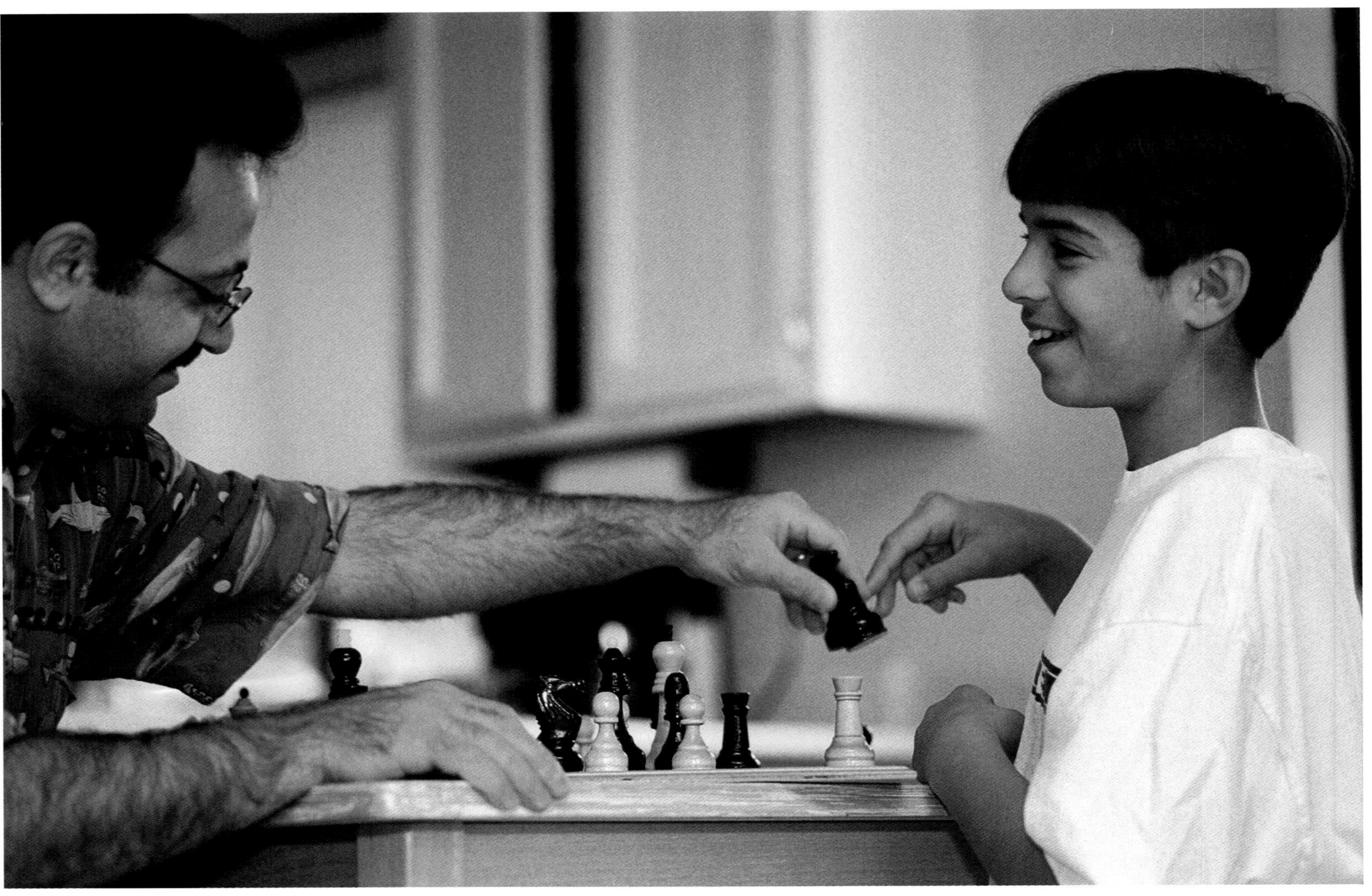

# *iranian*

SAJA PARVIZIAN, AGE 12

*"Oakland is really nice,"*
*says Saja. "It has a lot of natural places to hang out in,*
*a lot of people.*
*Most of my friends are pretty cool.*
*I choose my friends by characteristics.*
*I don't want friends*
*who will get me into trouble."*

*On being Iranian, Saja says,*
*"I like Islam. It's not complicated.*
*It has basic rules.*
*I like the food of my culture—it's really good."*

*Saja remembers his native country well,*
*especially the time he visited his grandpa.*
*"I would sit on his lap and we would talk.*
*He made me feel like I was*
*the most special kid in the world."*

# *chilean*

NATASHA SANTANDER, AGE 11

*Natasha immigrated*
*three years ago from Temuco, Chile,*
*where "it's cold*
*and everything's expensive,"*
*she says,*
*"but it's a beautiful environment...*
*no buildings*
*and not a lot of people."*

*She likes hiking,*
*camping, and winter skiing,*
*especially at Lake Tahoe.*
*"I want to be exploring around*
*the world like on one of the*
*TV nature shows.*
*I like it when you feel free in nature."*

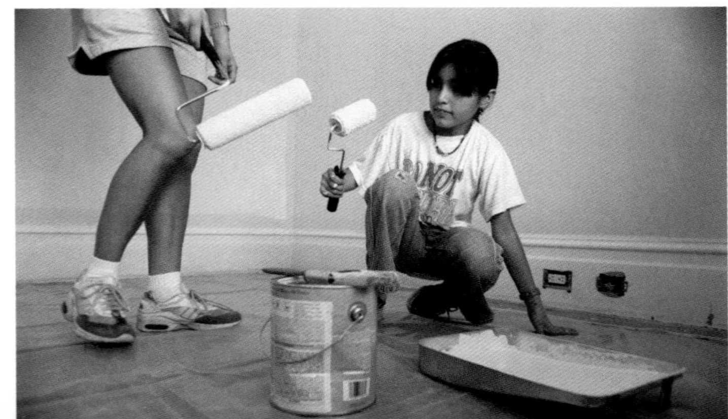

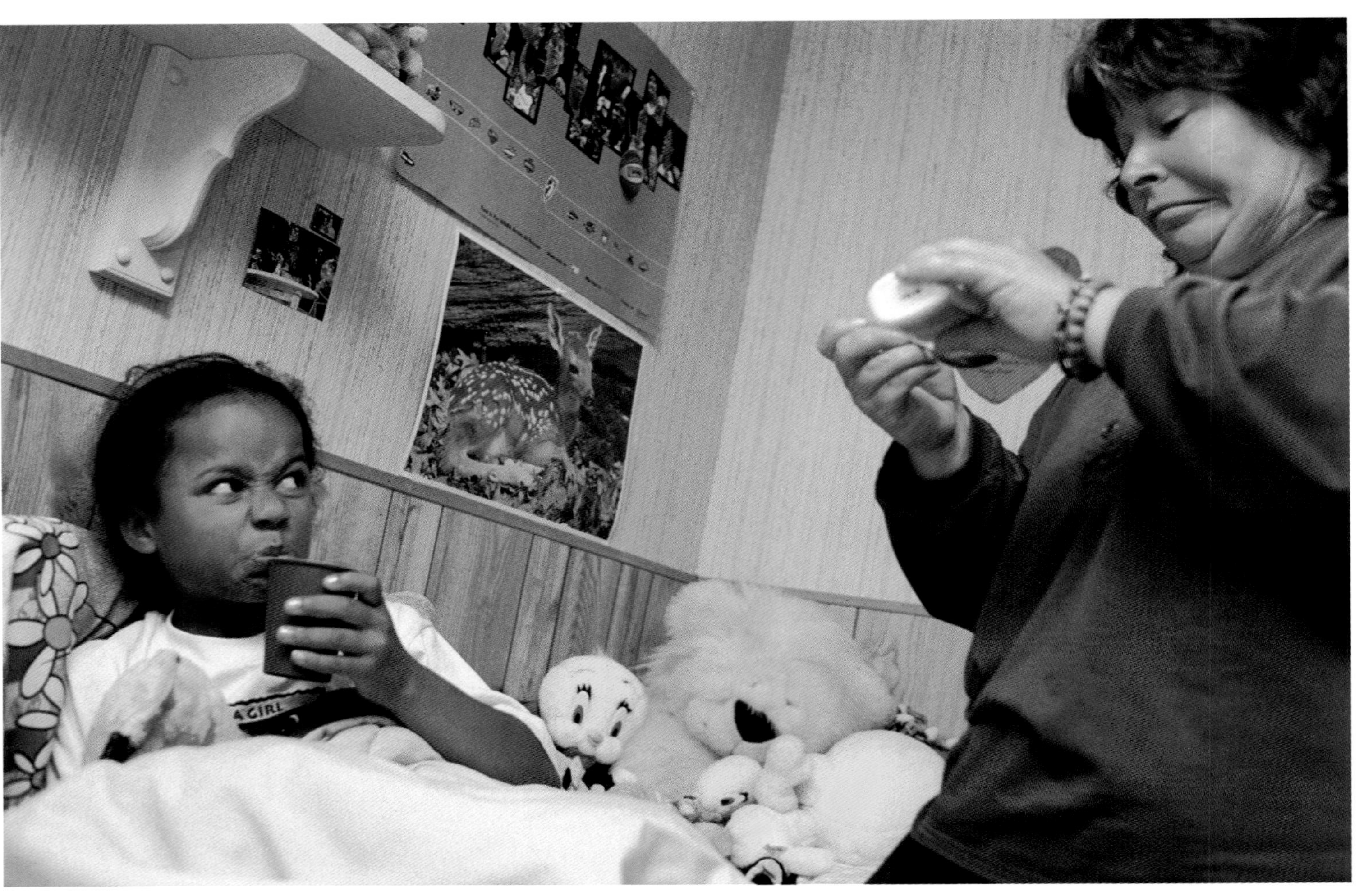
GIRL

*Lena (on facing page and below,*
*second from right)*
*likes all the "stuff" she can do*
*in Oakland,*
*like meeting a friend at*
*Happy Belly Deli*
*who became a "soulmate"*
*and riding her bike at*
*Mills College.*
*"School is also fun*
*—there are lots of fun things to do,*
*and there are*
*really good teachers."*

*Basketball camp*
*holds favorite-memory status:*
*"The best part was when*
*I made a backboard shot from*
*far away," says Lena.*
*"The whole game stopped."*

# ukrainian-lebanese

## Lena Kristina Greenspan, age 7

# *african american*

KATINA FEAZELL, AGE 7

*"I like my clothes*
*and my hair*
*—my momma does it pretty.*
*I like being a girl.*

*"I also like to play with*
*my three sisters,*
*three brothers, and cousins*
*—I love them.*

*"And I like to read*
*Arthur and*
*Clifford books."*

# eskimo–tlingit

## Alfredo Didrickson, age 13

*"I like being Eskimo because I'm different from most people,"*
*says Alfredo (right, with his younger brother).*
*He likes native dancing and art and would like to become a famous artist*
*of polar bears, dancers, walruses, and whales.*
*Alfredo even won $75 for artwork entered in a Native American art festival.*

*Monica's father*
*is Laguna and Navajo,*
*and her mother*
*is Filipino–Hawaiian.*
*"I like my*
*cultural background,"*
*she says.*
*"I like my skin color,*
*my long hair,*
*and the talents my parents*
*gave me. I have*
*a creative mind to construct*
*my own art,*
*whether it's painting or music.*

*"The best way*
*I can think of to make a mark*
*in the world*
*is through music," Monica says.*
*"I want the world to know*
*how much I appreciate the art.*
*The key is listening.*
*You can feel the music."*

# native american–filipino–hawaiian

MONICA SPENCER, AGE 13

# *belarusian*

MOLLY ANTONINA GALVIN, AGE 5

*Oakland's Lake Merritt*
*holds a special attraction*
*for Molly*
*(on facing page and*
*at left, center).*
*"I like to look out at the lake*
*and see the boats*
*and ducks," she says.*

*Her favorite place is*
*Children's Fairyland,*
*and the puppet theater*
*in particular.*
*"I want to be an actress.*
*I like to play*
*Peter Pan and Sleeping Beauty."*
*The best part*
*of Sleeping Beauty,*
*Molly says,*
*is when the prince*
*sings his song and holds*
*Sleeping Beauty's finger.*

Skyha

# *honduran*

MATTHEW BOHNSACK, AGE 10

*Although he was disappointed on this day*
*because a friend couldn't play with him,*
*Matt says he "feels really good about being me*
*because nothing really bad happens to me*
*and because I'm really smart."*

*Matt's best memories are of helping a little dog*
*find its owner and of the last time*
*he spent with his cat Andrew before he died.*
*What he hopes for most is that the two cats he has now,*
*Meow and Persian,*
*will be okay outside in the dark.*

# *jordanian*

ALEX TELHAMI, AGE 7

*Family comes first for Alex (center)*
*and his siblings.*
*"They never eat something*
*without sharing with each other,"*
*says his mother.*
*The children's schoolteachers*
*have told Mrs. Telhami*
*that they've never seen*
*brothers and sisters*
*love each other so much.*
*"The teachers said they feed each other,*
*help each other."*

*Alex says*
*he wants to be a builder of bridges,*
*houses, cars, and trains.*
*"Then I'll have lots of money*
*and can skip work*
*for a couple of days and spend time*
*with my family."*

# *greek*

## William Aristotle Damaskos, age 7

*William (right) engages in a little Pokémon card trading before assuming his responsibilities as an altar boy one Sunday at the Greek Orthodox Cathedral of the Ascension. "I have to wear a robe and yoke," says William. "I carry a candle, the cross, and incense."*

*He also participates in the church's dance and basketball programs. "I like my Greek dance, although the music is always too fast," he says, "and I like to play basketball. I won the league championships."*

*William keeps in touch with his five godbrothers in Athens by sending pictures and e-mail to them.*

# *laotian*

Anna Soundara, age 10

*Anna (center) has several friends from different countries,*
*and she tries to learn all their languages.*
*"They're really hard to say at first," she says.*
*"It takes a long time to learn,*
*but then they're really easy. I know Spanish a little,*
*Thai, Mien, and Chinese a little bit.*

*"I feel good that I get to go to school and learn,*
*and run around and have fun,*
*and I have a brain that I'm proud of and that I do stuff with it.*
*I want to learn much better,*
*and I want our school to get more textbooks."*

POWER

# PHOTOGRAPHER'S NOTES

*All photographs were taken by Marianne Thomas between March 14, 1999, and July 16, 2000.*

- 3 - **SAMOAN**

Mary Taylor oils up her nephew Danikko Taylor, 6, for his performance with the family dance group at the Oakland Asian Cultural Center's Polynesian festival. Danikko's cousin Robert Taylor, 7, who also dances, pokes his head into the scene.

- 4 - **TRINIDADIAN**

Merissa Lyons (far left), 9, swings with her friend Alia Phelps, 12, at DeFremery Park before a Juneteenth performance of Mas Makers Massive, a Trinidadian troupe in which they both dance.

- 7 - **GERMAN**

Finn T. Liss, 8, searches for guppies in a pond at Mills College late one Sunday afternoon. The Liss family lives on campus, where Finn's father, Fred Frith, teaches composition in the music department.

- 8 - **MEXICAN**

Miguel Nuño (center), 6, gets help with his tie as his kindergarten class prepares for its performance during Cinco de Mayo festivities at Lazear Elementary School. Dalia Michel (left), 6, and Anara Alvarez, 5, are ready to go.

- 10, 11 - **BRAZILIAN**

*Left-hand page:* At home, Annie Storey (left), 6, and her friend Lily Viek, 7, snack on avocados and paint their nails.
*Right-hand page:* Annie lends her jacket to Camille Hooks, 3, during Henry J. Kaiser, Jr. Elementary School's walkathon fund-raiser.

- 12, 13 - **KOREAN**

*Left-hand page:* April Kim, 10, practices a side kick during a tae kwon do class at an Oakland studio. She and her brother, Sean, 12, work out three times a week. *Right-hand page:* April and Sean serve themselves *shabu shabu*—a traditional Korean dish of thinly sliced beef dipped in fish broth and wrapped with rice in lettuce—at the grand opening of Jong Ga House, a Korean restaurant on Grand Avenue in Oakland.

- 15 - **FILIPINO**

Jeffrey Andrade, 8, and his sister Janice, 10, take a break from their after-school play to munch on bananas given to them by a neighbor who was on his way home from the corner store.

- 16 - BOSNIAN

Sanda Isakovic celebrates her sixth birthday with (from left) her friend Alisa Kapic, 12, and her sisters Sabina, 1, and Selma, 8.

- 18, 19 - NIGERIAN

*Left-hand page:* While waiting for their mother, Edosa Enagbare-Ona (left), 5, and his brothers, Osayaba (center), 9, and Osaru (right), 2, play on the bars at a check-cashing store. *Right-hand page:* Edosa plays video games at home one Saturday after shooting baskets at the East Lake YMCA.

- 20 - BELIZEAN

St. Jarlath team member Jennifer Hyde (left), 6, from Belize, joins St. Lawrence O'Toole's Jordan Gibbs (center), 8, and St. Leo's Isabella Avila Borgeson (right), 9, for a relay race during a track meet at St. Mary's College High School in Albany.

- 23 - GAMBIAN

Bakary Milon, 5, squeals with delight as he rolls his toy cars off the back porch.

- 24, 25 - GUATEMALAN AND COLOMBIAN

*Left-hand page and right-hand page, top:* Like siblings everywhere, Tony Young, 8, from Guatemala, and his sister, Marcela, 11, from Colombia, vacillate between the closeness that comes from reading to each other and the distance of the big tease. *Right-hand page, bottom:* Marcela holds Angie, their 1-year-old border collie mix, on the way home from a run on the grounds of Merritt College.

- 27 - SALVADORAN

Wilmer Antonio Callejas, 10, a recent arrival from El Salvador, alternates between quietness and exuberant activity as he adjusts to life in the United States. He is staying at a temporary home sponsored by the Catholic Church until his family can relocate.

- 28 - MIEN

From top, Lorie Saechin, 7, Nai Saechao, 9, and May Saeteurn, 7, listen to a Bible story during Sunday-school class at Oakland's Yiu-Mienh Baptist Church.

- 31 - EASTERN EUROPEAN JEWISH

On this particular Friday, Ilana Hannah Wexler, 8, wishes her *bubbe* (which means "grandma" in Yiddish) a happy birthday, as well as *Shabbat shalom* ("greetings on the Sabbath"). Ilana phones her grandmother every Friday before the family's Sabbath celebration.

- 32 - CAMBODIAN

From left, Ryan Kong, 8, Charlie Thoeung, 8, and Charath Kong, 4, play basketball in the courtyard of their apartment building in Oakland's Fruitvale district. Despite the boarded-up windows and run-down conditions, the children find ways to amuse themselves.

- 35 - INDIAN

When Rahul Singh Rao, 8, hangs out at his father's Breads of India and Gourmet Curries restaurant in Berkeley, he gets to sample the fare. Here, Rao Rohit Singh helps his son cut the large prawns they just cooked together in the restaurant kitchen. In the background is waiter Balwinder Singh (no relation).

- 36, 37 - NICARAGUAN

*Left-hand page:* Niquirana Hicks Rodriguez, 9, gets special treatment on the day of her First Holy Communion. She and her friends, including Jeimy Salazar (left), 9, and Mollie Roark (right), 9, ride to and from St. Elizabeth Church in a limo rented by her mom. *Right-hand page:* At top, Niki leaves the altar after giving a reading during the mass; at bottom, she takes a bow after stopping off at a multicultural festival at Thornhill Elementary School, where she attends third grade.

- 39 - THAI

Abby Bouaphavong, 10, practices backstage before a performance of her dance troupe at a Thai festival in San Francisco's Golden Gate Park.

- 40, 41 - LIBERIAN

*Left-hand page:* Terisha Charlene Harris (left), 11, escapes the repercussions of teasing neighbor Maijjai Jackson, 8, in front of her Oakland home while her mother, Bendu Griffin, looks on. *Right-hand page:* During a Bible-based motivational skills class led by her mother, Terisha portrays King Nebuchadnezzar's statue while her mom and the rest of the class pretend to be the Israelites, who must pay homage or be thrown into the fiery furnace.

- 43 - PARAGUAYAN

Talia Chess (left), 6, gets a lazy Sunday morning caress from her mother, Jan Chess, while her Guatemalan sister, Alana, 2, zips by.

- 44, 45 - ERITREAN

*Left-hand page:* Roabel Medhanie, 7, lets out a giggle during basketball practice at the Greek Orthodox Cathedral of the Ascension in Oakland. *Right-hand page:* Roabel passes the time with his sister Meron, 11, at a coffee shop in Montclair Village while they wait for a treat of bagels and cream cheese.

- 46, 47 - CHINESE-JAPANESE-VIETNAMESE

*Left-hand page:* While waiting in line to swing on the trapeze during gym class, Hope Setsuko Cooc (third from left), 7, tells her brother, Derrick Tsuyuki Cooc, 8, to shape up. They participate in the class at University Village Recreation in Albany with Joshua Lowhurst (left), 6; Camille Manansala Garnett (to right of Hope), 7; Jessica Peckham, 7; and Meredith Tsang, 8. *Right-hand page:* Hope explores part of her heritage with her father, Sau Quay Cooc, at a Chinese New Year's street festival in San Francisco before the traditional parade.

- 48 - **IRANIAN**

Saja Parvizian, 12, plays chess with his father, Mehdi Parvizian. Occasionally, including on this Saturday afternoon, Saja wins.

- 50, 51 - **CHILEAN**

*Left-hand page:* At bottom, Natasha Santander, 11, compares her small roller to the larger one held by her mother, Ester Vines, while they help paint the walls of a friend's Berkeley house, soon to be their new home; at right, Natasha and her grandmother Irene Soto Mella, visiting from Chile, walk to a self-service laundry on a wet Saturday morning to pick up the wash. *Right-hand page:* Natasha shoots some hoops into a plastic crate behind the Oakland Catholic Worker house where she and her mother are staying temporarily.

- 52, 53 - **UKRAINIAN-LEBANESE**

*Left-hand page:* Lena Kristina Greenspan, 7, gets a slug of some nasty-tasting homeopathic cough syrup from her mother, Helen Greenspan, just before going to bed. *Right-hand page:* On the last day of basketball camp at Mills College, Lena (second from right) cheers on her teammates during a final scrimmage. Fellow camp participants are (from left) Danielle Victoria Keenan, 9; Maddy Conboy, 10; and (at right) Sophia Albertini, 10.

- 55 - **AFRICAN AMERICAN**

Katina Feazell, 7, spends a school-day afternoon jumping rope on the patio outside her apartment building.

- 56 - **ESKIMO-TLINGIT**

Alfredo Didrickson, 13, gives his brother, Antonio, 3, a bike ride around Lake Merritt. The brothers are Tlingit on their father's side and Eskimo on their mother's.

- 59 - **NATIVE AMERICAN—FILIPINO-HAWAIIAN**

Monica Spencer, 13, takes a break from playing a wood block during a musical jam session at a family party one Sunday afternoon. Monica also plays the clarinet.

- 60, 61 - **BELARUSIAN**

*Left-hand page:* Molly Antonina Galvin, 5, waits for her friends to arrive for brunch on the day of the Million Mom March against guns. *Right-hand page:* After attending the rally with their mothers on a drizzling Sunday, Molly (center) and her playmates stop on their trek home to watch the geese at Lake Merritt.

- 62 - **HONDURAN**

Matthew Bohnsack's day starts badly when some of his friends cancel a play date at the last minute. His mother, Carol Bohnsack, comforts the 10-year-old, then takes him out for a hot dog and some shopping. Later, he caught up with a fellow video-game aficionado, and the tears dried up.

- 65 - JORDANIAN

While Alex Telhami (center), 7, watches television one Friday evening, his sister Kristina, 5, and brother, Kristopher, 2, circle playfully.

- 66 - GREEK

William Aristotle Damaskos (right), 7, trades Pokémon cards with Christopher Chriest, 7, before Sunday services at the Greek Orthodox Cathedral of the Ascension. In the background, Reverend Thomas J. Paris prepares for mass.

- 69 - LAOTIAN

Sisters Sissy Boungunha (left), 6, and Anna Soundara (center), 10, with their friend Dorithy Keomany (right), 12, wade in Sausal Creek after an Easter egg hunt at Dimond Park.

# CULTURAL TRADITIONS

*The following traditions are those represented by the children in this book. The cultural identifications were provided by the children's parents.*

**African American**

On June 19, 1865, two and a half years after President Abraham Lincoln signed the Emancipation Proclamation, slaves in Texas finally gained their freedom. Every year on that date, African Americans observe Juneteenth in many cities across the United States to honor those who persevered through the atrocities of slavery; it is a legal holiday in Texas. Juneteenth activities include parades (the Black Cowboys Association is a main feature of the Oakland parade), picnics, African American music, dance, literature, art, and storytelling. This is a day to celebrate the sacrifices and achievements of all African Americans.

**Belarusian**

Kupala (or Kupalle) is the Belarusian version of the midsummer festival, or summer solstice, although it is celebrated in early July. On Kupala night, young people go to the forests and meadows wearing flower garlands and dance in *karagods* (circles around a campfire). One of Belarus's greatest writers, Yanka Kupala (1882–1942), took his pen name from this holiday.

**Belizean**

Bicyclists come from all over the Caribbean and the United States to participate in the annual Belize Cross Country Race. Marvin Hyde, father of Jennifer Hyde (pages 20–21), looks forward to riding in this race every year. It starts in Belize City, the capital, and passes through about 50 villages, covering 144 miles and taking about six hours to complete. The first rider to pass through a village on the route receives a station prize contributed by the town council. The prize may be a bull, money, or a trophy.

**Bosnian**

During the Muslim month of Ramadan, the Isakovic family (pages 16–17) observes 30 days of fasting from sunrise to sunset. This period is followed by three days of celebration, called Bajram (bye-rahm), during which they wear new clothes, give gifts to others, shoot off fireworks, and hold parties. Baklava is a traditional sweet pastry made for this special occasion. Each person is greated with "Bajram-mu-barek" and responds with "Alla razile." These greetings convey happiness for the end of Ramadan and thankfulness to Allah.

**Brazilian**

St. John's Day, June 24, is a harvest celebration in Brazil. Little boys sell roasted corn on the street, children wear farmer clothes, and people paint mustaches on their faces with burnt cork. Bonfires are held in rural areas, and people stay up late at night, often setting off fireworks meant to wake St. John from sleep. (In many countries, this midsummer holiday commemorates St. John's prophecy that his own light would grow dimmer as Christ's light increased. John was born six months before Jesus, and the sun gets increasingly dimmer in the six months after John's birth and increasingly brighter in the months after Jesus' birth.)

**Cambodian** Cambodian New Year is celebrated during the new moon near the beginning of April. "Cambodian New Year is my favorite holiday," says Ryan Kong (pages 32–33). "We pray, put food on the table for our ancestors, and go to the temple to honor the people who passed away. And the food! It's good! We eat Cambodian food—some noodles, some curry, *nom sohm* [sweet rice and pork wrapped in banana leaves]. Other people come to visit and see how we're doing. We play Cambodian games. In *ja cho,* the guys stand on one side and the girls stand on the other. The guys throw a towel and if the girls can catch it, they make the boys sing and the girls get to dance. If the girls throw the towel and the boys can catch it, the girls have to sing and we get to dance."

**Chilean** On Chilean Independence Day, September 18, every restaurant, every house, everywhere, cooks meat pies called *empanadas.* People gather under large, outdoor arbors for music, barbecue, and *chieaa,* which is like apple cider. Children dress in the typical outfit of farmers, and everyone dances the traditional *la cueca.*

**Chinese** In a Chinese wedding, the bride usually changes clothes three times: from a white dress symbolizing purity, to a red silk dress symbolizing wealth and love, to a very formal dress welcoming motherhood. The succession of dresses symbolizes her stages of maturity: from little girl, to bonded adult, to mother.

**Colombian** One of the world's most beautiful public spectacles is Medellín's Desfile de los Silleteros ("The Carriers' Parade"), held every August. For this event, hundreds of Colombian artisans weave flowers into tapestries that tell stories and carry these colorful works of art on their backs for hours through the streets of the city.

**Eastern European Jewish** Shabbat, the Jewish Sabbath, begins each Friday evening with the lighting of candles at sundown and ends at sundown Saturday. It is a time for rest, contemplation, and prayer after a busy week. It is also a time to appreciate the miracle of the world created by God in six days. After a blessing, challah (egg bread) and wine are shared.

**Eritrean** Eritrean Festival is held in ten major cities worldwide during August to promote unity among the nine different Eritrean nationalities and to help youngsters stay in touch with their culture. This three-day festival is filled with teaching, dance, sports, music, and art by the young and old. In 1999, Oakland was one of the festival's host cities, and more than 10,000 people attended the event.

**Eskimo and Tlingit** The Eskimo and Tlingit cultures in Alaska are geographically close to one another and share some similar traditions, such as artistry. Eskimos are carvers of ivory, and Tlingit people are carvers of totem poles and canoes. Animals are like brothers and sisters to people of these cultures. The Tlingit still hunt the way their ancestors did, performing ritual ceremonies beforehand to show respect for the animals. The Tlingit tribe has two major divisions, the ravens and the eagles, who marry each other. The clans in these divisions are named after other animal species.

**Filipino** Piesta is a joyous celebration held by families and communities throughout the Philippines beginning at midnight on April 27 to commemorate their cities' patron saints. Mr. Andrade, father of Jeffrey Andrade (pages 14–15), is from the city of La Paz, which celebrates the miraculous appearance of St. Nuestra de la Paz. Families attend church the morning of April 28, visit friends, participate in baseball and basketball competitions, and join in dancing. Lots of movies are shown, and parades fill the streets.

**Gambian** Tubaske is celebrated by Muslims in Gambia for one week after the end of Ramadan. On the first morning, each family prays and then sacrifices a lamb to cleanse their sins. They then take gifts of charity to neighbors and spend the remainder of the week feasting.

**German** Lanterna, or St. Martinstag, is celebrated in southern and western Germany on November 11 in remembrance of St. Martin of Tours, a fourth-century Roman soldier who was appointed bishop because of his good deeds (which included rending his cloak in two and giving half to a beggar freezing in the cold). Children parade through the streets with lanterns and sing in front of houses about the generosity of St. Martin, for which they are rewarded with candy, money, and hot chocolate. The lanterns are often handmade from hollowed-out beets and have faces carved into them. Some parades feature a "real" St. Martin on a horse.

**Greek** Name Day, a birthday-like celebration of the saint for whom a person is named, is an important tradition in Greek culture. William Damaskos (pages 66–67) was named after St. Vassilios (Basil), which translates as William; therefore, William and his family celebrate St. Basil's Day, on January 1. On that day, they go to church and then eat a family dinner that includes St. Basil's bread *(vasilopita),* which is baked with a coin in it. According to tradition, whoever gets the piece of bread with the coin in it will receive many blessings in the year to come. The practice of baking coins, or even jewels, in bread and distributing the loaves to poor families on this day is based on stories that St. Basil, who was a bishop around A.D. 370, would bring coins or oranges to children.

**Guatemalan** On Christmas Eve, Guatemalans set off firecrackers at midnight, open presents, eat tamales, and drink *ponche,* a hot drink made from fresh and dried fruits.

**Hawaiian** May Day, celebrated on May 1, is a day for family and friends to gather and prepare flower necklaces called leis. Different types and colors of flowers are used to make the leis, according to the family's island of origin. The entire day is devoted to picking the flowers, creating the leis, and draping them over each other. On the Big Island, a parade is usually held, and leis are hung over the statue of King Kamehameha. Luaus (Hawaiian feasts) and dances follow. Before U.S. colonization, it was the men who danced. Now, it is usually the women.

**Honduran** Hondurans in the capital city of Tegucigalpa observe Santa Semana (Holy Week) processions, which are held every day from Palm Sunday to Easter Sunday. The processions include the Triumphal Arrival of Christ into Jerusalem, the Procession of Chains, the Holy Burial, and the Procession of the Empty Tomb. In smaller towns, Hondurans still build *descansos,* or rest stops, with altars and decorate the processional path with *alfombras,* elaborate carpets made of colored sawdust.

**Indian** India's Festival of Lights, Diwali, is held in the fall to celebrate the return of the Hindu deity Lord Rama after 14 years of exile. Families light candles and oil lamps in their houses, perform religious ceremonies, exchange gifts, set off fireworks, visit friends, and go to the temple.

**Iranian** Eid Noroz, the Iranian New Year celebration, is held on the first day of spring. Family members gather in thankfulness for gifts from God, and a table is decorated with seven objects beginning with the letter *s* and symbolizing life, health, beauty, and happiness. For instance, sprouted lentils, bundled and wrapped with ribbon, are displayed as a symbol of life and growth.

**Japanese** A Japanese bride usually wears a white wedding gown and then changes for the reception and tea ceremony to a white satin kimono with headpiece and special slippers. An experienced staff of five people can help her make the change in one hour; otherwise, the clothing change may take up to three hours.

**Jordanian** For Alex Telhami (pages 64–65) and his family, the Christian holidays are especially meaningful times to gather together and honor their heritage. Telhami means "from Bethlehem" in Arabic. Two hundred years ago, Alex's great-great-grandfather immigrated to Nazareth, and now an entire clan of Telhamis lives there. Alex and his sister Kristina were baptized at the Church of the Nativity, widely recognized as the birthplace of Christ, by a priest who is their relative.

**Korean** On Korean New Year, children bow to their parents and grandparents as a sign of respect and wish them health and happiness. The elders give the younger ones gifts of money for good luck and blessing.

**Laotian** Laotians prepare for their new year, called Boon Pee Mai, in the fifth lunar month, usually April, with a unique ritual of washing away the old year and welcoming the new. As much as two weeks before the celebration begins, people throw water on each other, either a sprinkling or a good dousing. Even houses and Buddha statues are ritually washed. Each family brings offerings of food, including special desserts, to the temple for three days during the celebration. One offering is for Buddha, one is for the ancestors, and one is for the Teveda, or angel, who is sent to protect people on earth and foretell what the new year will hold. Dancing and feasting follow.

**Liberian** Dancing is an important Liberian tradition. The dances tell stories about life—birth, death, marriage, happiness, sadness. Dance is a means of worship and even of exorcism. "When I hear drums, my feet start moving," says Bendu Griffin, mother of Terisha Harris (pages 40–41). "Dance is a means of communicating." Different tribes, groups, women, and individuals have different dances to tell their stories.

**Mexican** The family of Miguel Nuño (pages 8–9) and other parents at Lazear Elementary School celebrate Cinco de Mayo—the defeat of France at the Battle of Puebla—with everybody cooking and selling Mexican food to raise money for the school. The children and the parents dance and sing. However, more is made of Cinco de Mayo in the United States than in Mexico, where it is a primarily a regional holiday. A tradition that is important throughout Mexico is El Día de los Muertos (The Day of the Dead), held November 1 and 2. (November 1, All Saints Day, is for deceased children; November 2, All Souls Day, is for deceased adults.) Ancient indigenous peoples of Mexico believed that the dead return each year to visit and celebrate with their relatives. Toys and balloons are placed on children's graves, and the favorite food and drink of the departed are prepared for adults' graves. The celebration also includes flowers, candies, candles, and incense shared by family members at the graves.

**Mien** Whether it be for a wedding or Mien New Year, women, men, and babies wear costumes that are elaborately and colorfully embroidered from head to toe in intricate designs that tell stories and take up to a year to prepare. One long strand of silver pieces—coins, fish, spiked balls, and other designs—is then wrapped around the head and another around the shoulders. When a costumed person walks, the silver swishes and makes a soothing, tinkling sound. Women also wrap their heads in turbans made with about three arm-spans of material. They use another wrap to carry babies up to 2 years old on their backs. The babies wear caps decorated differently according to their gender.

**Native American** Many native peoples of the Americas, and those who stand in solidarity with them, celebrate Indigenous Peoples Day the Saturday before Columbus Day. This day focuses the world's attention on the history of European subversion of native peoples in the Americas. In Northern California, Berkeley and Alcatraz Island are two hosts of Indigenous Peoples Day observances, with a sunrise service on Alcatraz, traditional powwows, and recognition of the Native Americans' past and present, especially the sacrifices and contributions of the ancestors. Monica Spencer (pages 58–59), for instance, is a member of the largest relocated family in Oakland. Her paternal grandmother and grandfather were stripped of everything and told to leave the Southwest. Monica's grandfather later lectured on Navajo culture at the University of California at Berkeley and Stanford University, and all his nine children attended college.

**Nicaraguan** Purissima, held December 1 through 8, is a national celebration commemorating the Immaculate Conception. Most households build an altar for the Virgin Mary for this week. On December 8, people attend church and then go door to door singing songs at the altars of each home and receiving candy. "Every child must receive *gofio,* a homemade candy of corn and honey," says Lissette Rodriguez, mother of Niki Hicks Rodriguez (pages 36–37), "or else it is not Purissima." Fireworks are shot off all day and night.

**Nigerian** Egwẹ is an important tradition among the Edo-speaking Bini tribe. On the eve of December 24, all the family gathers to give thanks for the year that has passed and to pray for protection in the coming year. Prayers are offered for each family member during a ceremony that includes a hen, coconut, kola nut, and *kankan,* an alcoholic drink that is similar to gin. The next morning, the hen is cooked along with pounded yam and *egusi,* a soup made from melon seeds and other ingredients. This food is shared among the family members as they sit and eat together.

**Paraguayan** Three Kings Day (the Feast of the Epiphany) is a joyous occasion celebrated on January 6 in remembrance of the arrival of the wise men, who were astronomers following the star to Jesus' birthplace. Paraguayans celebrate this day with festivals, parties in the streets, and gift giving throughout the day and into the night.

**Salvadoran** Salvador del Mundo ("Savior of the World"), August 6, is a day that Salvadorans honor Jesus. Adults and children participate in processions in cities and throughout the countryside. Since the capital city, San Salvador, is central in this small country, many people travel there to join its procession and to attend a special mass.

**Samoan** On Samoan Flag Day, Samoans honor King Malietoa and Queen Salamasina and the high chiefs with a parade, food, dance, and rugby. The father and grandfather of Danniko Taylor (pages 2–3) are high chiefs, each bearing the name of Leota Toleafoa.

**Thai** King Bhumibol's birthday, December 5, is one of many favorite celebration days for Thai people. The king is the longest-reigning Thai monarch, and he and his wife, Queen Sirikit, are deeply revered. Since the king is the symbolic father of all Thai people, this day is also celebrated as Father's Day. People decorate their homes and businesses, light candles while singing a song to the king, and set off fireworks. Abby Bouaphavong (pages 38–39) performs Thai dances at the temple on this day and for other festivals.

**Trinidadian** Carnival is a no-holds-barred celebration held right before Lent, the 40 days during which observers abstain from worldly pleasures in preparation for Easter. Trinidad's Carnival is one of the largest celebrations in the world, with steel pan orchestras (Trinidad invented the steel drum) and elaborately dressed dancers parading through the streets. Dancers costumed as various caricatures act out traditional stories. The costumes, representing characters such as Dame Lorraine (which satirizes the French colonizers), burrokeet (the faithful burro), and Jab Molassie (the devil), are often passed down through family generations.

**Ukrainian-Lebanese** Lena Greenspan (pages 52–53) especially enjoys the Jewish celebration of Hanukkah "because I get to spin the dreidel. I also like the latkes—they're potato pancakes—and lighting the menorah." Also, at the Passover seder, she likes to sing the traditional songs and to taste the parsley dipped in salt water, which represents the bitter experiences and the tears of the Hebrew people.

**Vietnamese** A Vietnamese wedding ceremony is performed at both the bride's and the groom's houses. The couple serves traditional tea or wine to the elders. The elders present red envelopes containing money to the couple, wishing them good luck, prosperity, fortune, and happiness.